KEITH EDWIN GRAHAM

Presents

The Songs of the Survivor

(Spiritual Beacons)

Inspired by God

The Songs of the Survivor

(Spiritual Beacons)

Inspired by God

COPYRIGHT PAGE

NAME OF BOOK: SONGS OF THE SURVIVOR
(SPIRITUAL BEACONS)

COPYRIGHT DATES: 2012, KEITH E. GRAHAM

ALL RIGHTS RESERVED. THIS PUBLICATION MAY NOT BE REPRODUCED OR QUOTED IN WHOLE OR IN PART IN PRINTED OR ELECTRONIC FORM, OR USED IN PRESENTATIONS, ON RADIO, TELE-VISION, VIDEOTAPE, FILM, OR OTHER ELECTRONIC MEANS WITHOUT WRITTEN PERMISSION FROM KEITH EDWIN GRAHAM.

WRITTEN BY: KEITH EDWIN GRAHAM

ISBN: 978-0-578-10975-6

PRINTED IN THE UNITED STATES

INTERIOR ARRANGEMENT AND FORMATTING
BY PAT KRISEL, PHOTOGRAPHIK

TO ORDER COPIES, PLEASE CONTACT -
KGRAHAM3869@YAHOO.COM

DEDICATION

This book is dedicated to the memory of my Great Grandmother, Phoebe H. Graham, my Grandfather, Roosevelt Graham Sr., and my brother, Bobby K. Pressley.

ACKNOWLEDGMENTS

First and foremost I give all the praise, honor and glory to God.
For God so loved the world that he gave his only begotten son, that whosoever believes in him should not perish but have everlasting life. John 3:16
I would like to give a special thank you to my children, Amira Graham, Keith Graham Jr., and Lauren Davis, for being the light in my life. I love each one of you with all my heart. And always remember in everything you do put God first. Thank you Grandmomma Essie Mae for always being there for me when no one else was, I love you.
Also thanks for Pastor John T. Miller, Rev. Mayso Porch and Rev. Ronald Williams and the entire congregation of Emanuel Baptist Church.
Thanks to Pamela Berry for steering me in the right direction from the beginning to the end.
Thanks to Pat and John Krisel at PhotoGraphik for putting God's work together in such a unique way.

CONTENTS

PART 1.   ALPHALIGHTS   1 THRU 25

PART 2.   BEACONS BRIGHT   26 THRU 50

PART 3.   CELESTIAL SIGHT   51 THRU 75

PART 4.   OMEGA'S MIGHT   76 THRU 100

CONTENTS
PART 1. ALPHALIGHTS

1. WHERE ARE WE
2. MORE THAN A MAN
3. BY FAITH
4. THE TOP
5. JESUS
6. WHO AM I
7. BACK UP SATAN
8. THE WAY
9. THE HALO
10. IF WE TRY
11. WHAT'S GOING ON
12. NEW WORLD ORDER
13. ON MY KNEES
14. WITHOUT A KEY
15. I AM LOVE
16. TRIALS
17. UNDEFEATABLE
18. THE DOCTOR
19. ADAM AND EVE
20. DARKNESS TO LIGHT
21. IMAGINE
22. WINDOWS
23. AWESOME
24. TRIAL OF FIRE
25. REFUGE

CONTENTS
PART 2. BEACONS BRIGHT

26. MUSTARD SEEDS
27. WHAT EVER
28. WHAT YOU SOW
29. I SAY YES
30. SHARE
31. MOTHER NATURE
32. JUST FOR YOU
33. NOT TOO LATE
34. STAND AND FIGHT
35. MY SAVIOR
36. OPEN THE DOORS
37. HOLY WATER
38. ORIGINAL SIN
39. MORE THAN CONQUERS
40. I ADORE
41. POWER
42. NO APPEAL
43. NO END
44. CHOSEN
45. TRUST ME
46. ARE YOU READY
47. NO DEBATE
48. LIFE INSURANCE
49. BLUEPRINT
50. A SHORT TIME

CONTENTS
PART 3. CELESTIAL SIGHT

51. FINAL PHASE
52. THE ROCK
53. THE FALLEN
54. THE PLOT
55. HEAR THIS
56. THE CLAIM
57. CAN'T KEEP ME DOWN
58. INTERVENTION
59. PERFECT PEACE
60. WORD OF GOD
61. DISBARRED
62. YIELD
63. THE TRINITY
64. MY SWEET RELIEF
65. THE DITCH
66. THE ZONE
67. MY SAFETY NET
68. IF YOU KNOCK
69. A TOWER
70. THE FOUNTAIN
71. ASCENSION
72. THE GAME
73. REDEMPTION
74. INSURRECTION
75. CIRCUS MONKEY

CONTENTS
PART 4. OMEGA'S MIGHT

76. ALPHA AND OMEGA
77. ENDORSEMENT
78. A LAMP
79. TICKING DOWN
80. MY QUARTERBACK
81. THE PURPOSAL
82. A JEWEL
83. THE SHOWDOWN
84. HOPE
85. SUPERNATURAL
86. THE REBIRTH
87. SONGS OF THE SURVIVOR
88. HOT LINE
89. INDEPENDENCE
90. THE SURVEY
91. WHAT'S INSIDE
92. PERFECT
93. COUNTER CLOCK
94. A JOURNEY
95. NOT ALONE
96. THE FAST LANES
97. SIGHT BEYOND SIGHT
98. THE SOLUTION
99. OUT HOUSE
100. NOT PROMISED

WHERE ARE WE

ABOVE THE SKIES WHERE I'LL BE FREE,

I WONDER IF THERE'S A PLACE FOR ME.

BEYOND THE GATES OF PETER'S KEY,

FOREVER HIS LIGHT FOR ME TO SEE.

LIFE FROM DEATH WAS MEANT TO BE,

HE SENT THE ONE WHO PAID YOUR FEE.

ABOVE THE EARTH NAILED TO A TREE,

ALL FOUND GUILTY WAS THE THREE.

TECHNO ADVANCEMENTS BUT WHERE ARE WE,

FIGHTING THE TERROR ACROSS THE SEA.

SOUND THE HORN THE ANGELS SING,

COMING SOON OUR LORD AND KING.

MORE THAN A MAN

CREATED MORE THAN JUST A MAN,

WORSHIPPING ON HIS KNEES AND HANDS.

ON HIS WORD IS HOW HE STANDS,

A MINISTER OF GOD ACROSS THE LANDS.

WRITTEN IN STONE IS HIS PLAN,

BREAK THE UNBREAKABLE IF YOU CAN.

TIME TO STOP RUNNING IF YOU RAN,

REMEMBER HE CARRIED YOU IN THE SAND.

BY FAITH

I COME THIS FAR BY FAITH,

DEEP IN WATERS TO THE WAIST.

STARING DEATH IN HIS FACE,

LIKE A TREE I WILL STAY IN PLACE.

SOUR GRAPES IS NOT MY TASTE,

SEEKING THE VICTORY IN THIS RACE.

WITHOUT GOD IT IS JUST A WASTE,

BURNING IN HELL WITHOUT A TRACE.

CHOOSE GOD NOW YOU WILL HAVE A CASE,

THE ONLY WAY IT IS THROUGH HIS GRACE.

THE TOP

THERE'S A PLACE I WANT TO GO,

MORE BEAUTIFUL THAN WINTERS SNOW.

THE PURE OF HEART WILL SURELY KNOW,

MASS OF BLUE GRASS WHERE FOUNTAINS FLOW.

MOUNTAINS HIGH AND MOUNTAINS LOW,

WHERE ANGELS FLY ALL IN A ROW.

EVERYONE IS EQUAL NO ONE BELOW,

ONLY LOVE IS ALLOWED TO GROW.

YOUR INVITED IF YOU WISH TO COME,

GOING TO THE TOP IS A LOT MORE FUN.

JESUS

THANK YOU GOD FOR ALL YOU HAVE DONE,

GIVING THE WORLD YOUR ONLY SON.

ALL OF HEAVEN ROLLED IN ONE,

TAKING THE LOAD THAT WEIGHS A TON.

UPON YOUR ARRIVAL THY KINGDOM COME,

YES THE BATTLE IS ALREADY WON!

WHO AM I

AGAINST ALL ODDS YOU MUST STAND,

TRUST IN ME YOU WILL NOT BE DAMNED.

IF YOU NEED I WILL TAKE YOUR HAND,

WHO AM I? THE GREAT I AM.

PONTIUS PILATE SUFFERED THE LAMB,

TAKING AWAY THE SINS OF MAN.

BACK UP SATAN

BACK UP SATAN GET OUT MY FACE,

NOT MY FAULT YOU FELL FROM GRACE.

REBELLED AND TRIED TO TAKE HIS PLACE,

THE WILL OF GOD WON'T BE ERASED.

BUILT ON LIES YOUR HOUSE IS BASED,

ARCHANGEL MICHAEL WILL KEEP ME SAFE.

THE WAY

PLEASE JESUS SHOW ME THE WAY,

TRYING TO MAKE IT ONE MORE DAY.

ALL I NEED IS FOR YOU TO SAY,

REST EASY MY CHILD IT WILL BE OK.

WITHIN MY MANSION IS WHERE YOU'LL STAY,

BY MY SIDE IS WHERE YOU'LL LAY.

THE HALO

ALL ABOARD THE HALO FOR
THE ADVENTURE OF YOUR LIFE,
ONE TOKEN OF LOVE FROM THE MAN
ABOVE THAT IS YOUR ONLY PRICE.
AN ANGEL FOOD FACTORY MADE OF
SUGARCANES HONEY AND SPICE,
THE VALLEY OF THE SAINTS IS CONSECRATED
IT WILL MAKE YOUR HEART BEAT TWICE.
A DOS-A-DOS DANCE CONDUCTED BY THREE
BLIND MICE,
WHERE COTTON CANDY CLOUDS PRODUCE
RAINBOW FLAVORED ICE.
JUST A LITTLE TASTE OF HEAVEN IT WOULD
BE VERY NICE,
BUT NOTHING CAN COMPARE TO THE DAY
WHEN I SEE THE FACE OF
CHRIST.

IF WE TRY

LEADERS WEARING SUITS AND TIE,

MARCH OUR SOLDIERS OFF TO DIE.

SPILLING BLOOD WHAT'S THE REASON WHY?

FAMILIES LOSING BACK HOME THEY CRY.

THIS MESSAGE IS FOR ALL SIDES,

A PEACE BETWEEN US WON'T HURT YOUR PRIDE.

DIFFERENCES WE CAN PUT TO THE SIDE,

EVERYONE UNITED IF WE TRY.

WHAT'S GOING ON

PUBLIC SCHOOL SHOOTINGS WHAT'S GOING ON,

NO PADDLE PUNISHMENTS THIS WAS WRONG.

THE OUR FATHER PRAYER EVEN THIS IS GONE,

STRUCTURE IS BROKEN SO IS OUR BOND.

INTERNET PREDATORS WE CAN'T BE CALM,

GUN CARRYING STUDENTS SOUND THE ALARM.

IT'S ALL ABOUT THE BLING ON YOUR ARM,

OUR CHILDREN IS GULLABLE TO THE WICKED CHARMS.

NEW WORLD ORDER

SENSELESS SLAUGHTER IN THE STREETS,

NEW WORLD ORDER OF THE BEAST.

HARDEN HEARTS WILL SIGN HIS LEASE,

HE IS SINKING DEEPER WITH HIS TEETH.

RAIN DOWN FIRE THIS WILL NOT CEASE,

ALL AROUND SUFFERING IS YOUR GRIEF.

WITHOUT CHANGE THERE IS NO PEACE,

IF YOU REJECT GOD YOU ARE SATAN'S FEAST.

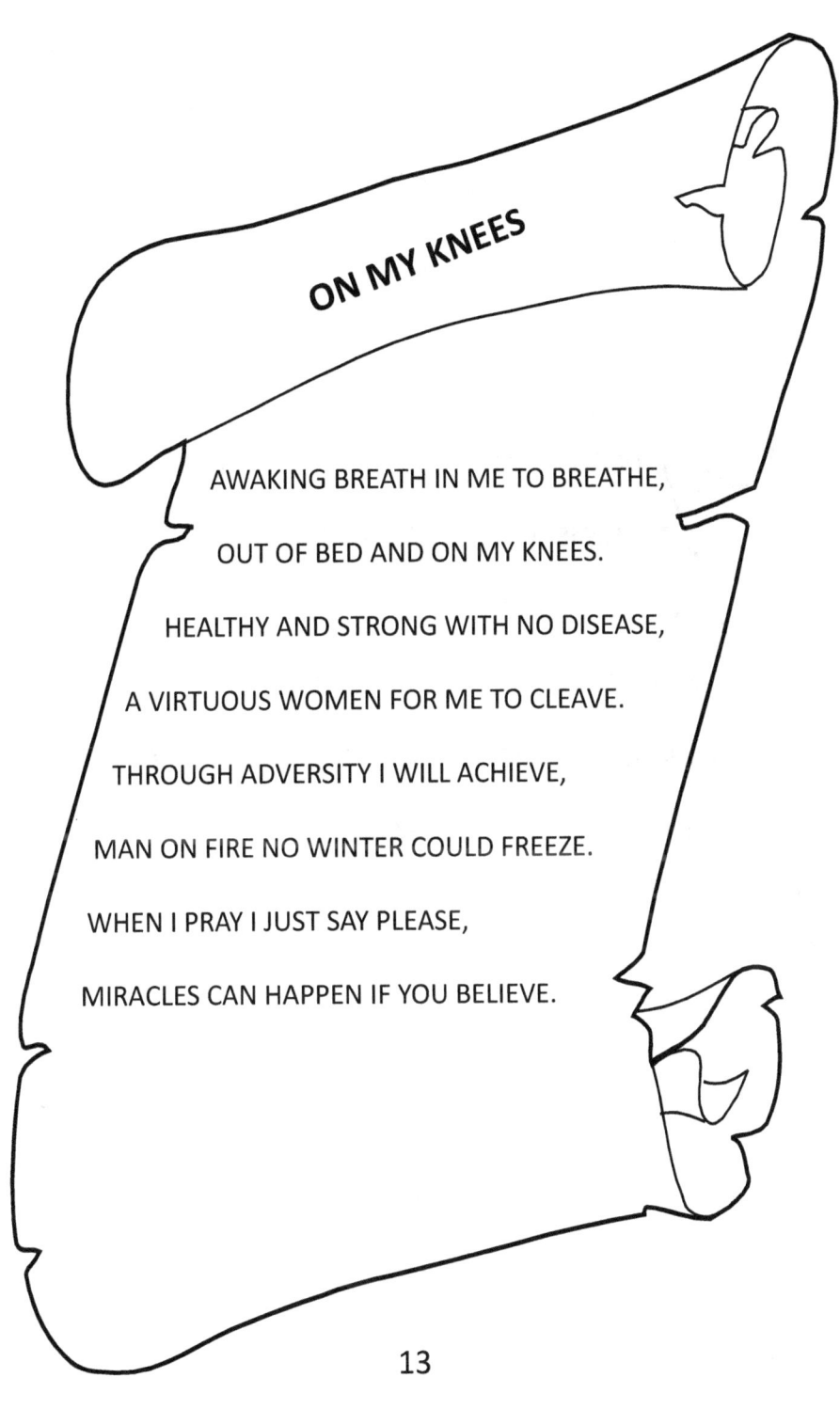

ON MY KNEES

AWAKING BREATH IN ME TO BREATHE,

OUT OF BED AND ON MY KNEES.

HEALTHY AND STRONG WITH NO DISEASE,

A VIRTUOUS WOMEN FOR ME TO CLEAVE.

THROUGH ADVERSITY I WILL ACHIEVE,

MAN ON FIRE NO WINTER COULD FREEZE.

WHEN I PRAY I JUST SAY PLEASE,

MIRACLES CAN HAPPEN IF YOU BELIEVE.

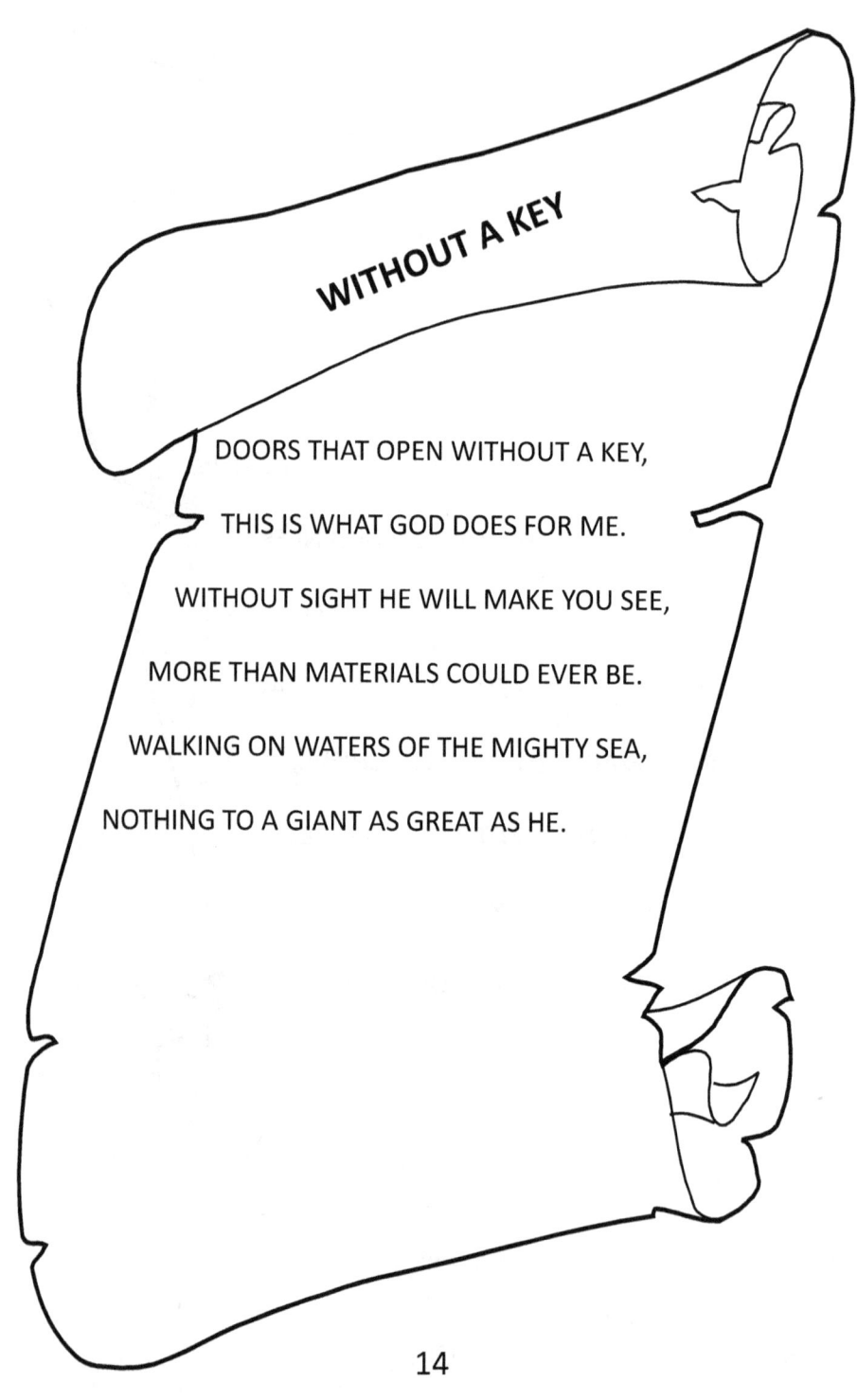

WITHOUT A KEY

DOORS THAT OPEN WITHOUT A KEY,

THIS IS WHAT GOD DOES FOR ME.

WITHOUT SIGHT HE WILL MAKE YOU SEE,

MORE THAN MATERIALS COULD EVER BE.

WALKING ON WATERS OF THE MIGHTY SEA,

NOTHING TO A GIANT AS GREAT AS HE.

I AM LOVE

I AM THE SHEPHERD OF THE SHEEP,

MY COMMANDMENTS THEY WILL KEEP.

I AM THE STRENGTH IN THE STRONG,

FULL ARMOR OF GOD NO WEAPON FORMED.

I AM THE SAVIOR OF THE SAVED,

THEY WALK THE ROADS THAT I HAVE PAVED.

I AM THE WISDOM IN THE WISE,

FOR THOSE WHO SEEK THE GREATEST PRIZE.

I AM ALL THE THINGS ABOVE,

TO PUT IT SIMPLY I AM LOVE.

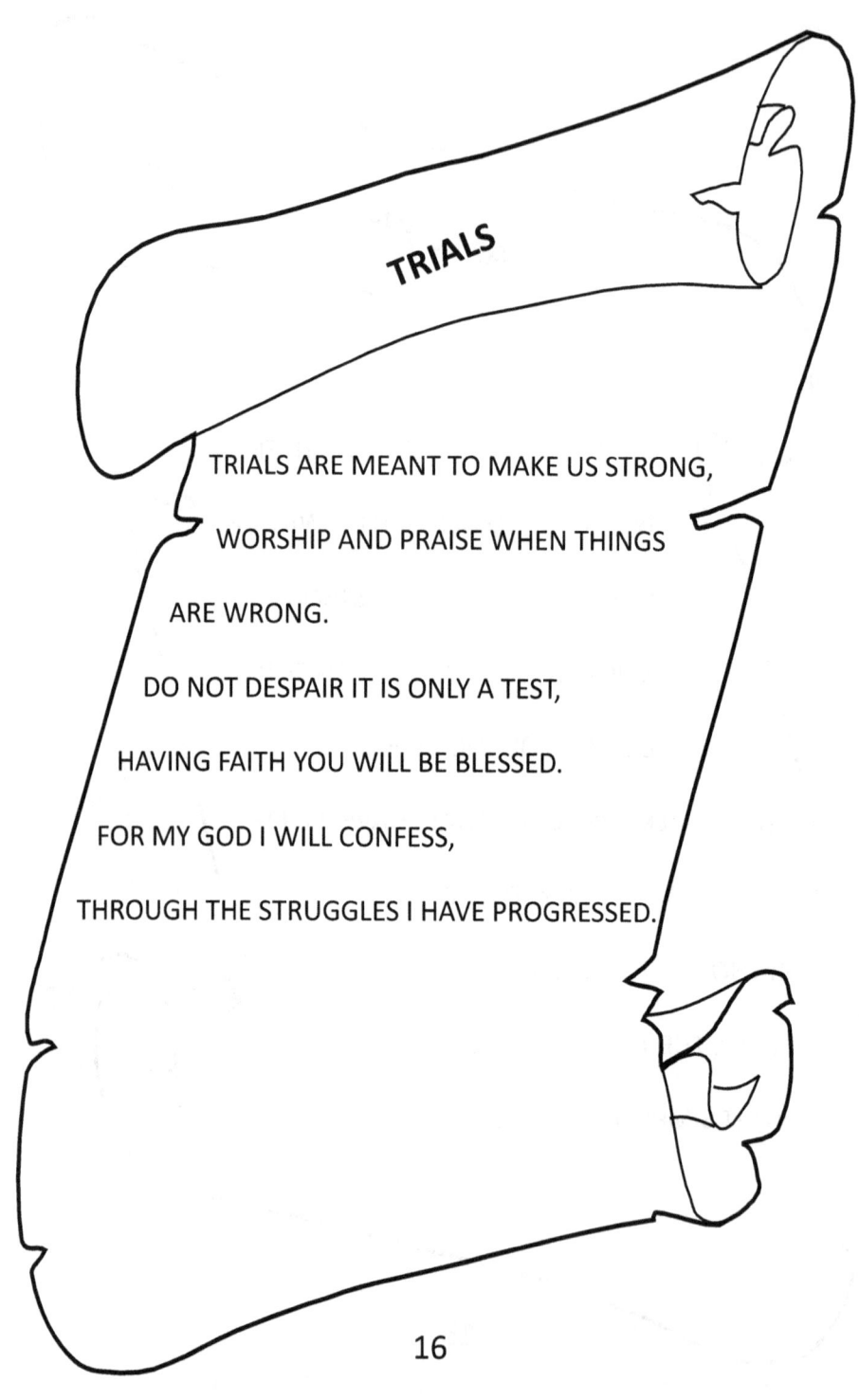

UNDEFEATABLE

UNDEFEATABLE IS A MAN,

WHO KEEPS THE WORD OF GOD IN HAND.

HE IS ALWAYS HUMBLE NEVER GRAND,

GIVES HIS LAST WHEN HE CAN.

MARK OF THE CHOSEN IS HIS BRAND,

TRIALS OF LIFE HE UNDERSTANDS.

THE DOCTOR

NEVER PROCLAIM THAT YOU ARE SICK,

KEEPING YOU DOWN IS SATAN'S TRICK.

DIAGNOSIS SAYS TO SEE HIM QUICK,

FIRST OPINION WHOM SHALL I PICK.

TOLD TO ME IS THE ONE WHO WOULDN'T

LEAVE US,

HE GOES BY THE NAME OF DOCTOR JESUS.

ADAM AND EVE

A MAN CALLED ADAM WAS THE FIRST,

PARADISE WAS HIS PLACE OF BIRTH.

GIVEN DOMINION OVER THE EARTH,

PRAISING GOD IS HIS WORTH.

LOYAL AND TRUE IN ALL HIS DEEDS,

CHOSEN FOR HIM A WIFE CALLED EVE.

BY THE SERPENT THEY WERE DECEIVED,

EYES WIDE OPEN BEHIND THE LEAVES.

DARKNESS TO LIGHT

LIGHT FROM DARKNESS, DARKNESS TO LIGHT.

FIGHTING TEMPTATIONS WITH ALL THY MIGHT.

STAYING THE COURSE I WILL DO WHAT'S RIGHT,

THIS MISSION FOR GOD I WILL KEEP IT TIGHT.

WHERE EVER THERE IS DARKNESS I WILL SHINE BRIGHT,

GIVING HIM HONOR IS WHY I WRITE.

IMAGINE

IMAGINE A PERFECT PLACE IN TIME,

A WONDROUS LAND WITH NO CRIME.

SUNNY DAYS THAT ALWAYS SHINE,

BROADWAY SHOWS DON'T COST A DIME.

TROPICAL FRUITS THAT TASTE LIKE WINE,

NO BLURRED VISIONS OF THE MIND.

THERE IS NO LEASE FOR YOU TO SIGN,

DIVE ON IN THE WATER IS FINE.

WINDOWS

THE EYES ARE WINDOWS TO THE SOUL,

ENCHANTED MYSTERIES I WAS TOLD.

SEAS OF TEARS IS WHAT THEY HOLD,

HAPPY OR SAD SOMETIMES THEY ROLL.

THEY ARE ABLE TO SEE INSIDE A HEART OF GOLD

FILLED WITH WISDOM WHEN THEY ARE OLD.

AWESOME

AWESOME IS THE GOD I SERVE,

RECEIVING BLESSINGS I DON'T DESERVE.

MY HEART AND SOUL HE HAS PRESERVE,

TO LIVE AGAIN IS WHAT I HEARD.

I AM LEANING ON HIS EVERY WORD,

MY COACH TO HEAVEN HAS BEEN RESERVED

TRIAL OF FIRE

THERE ARE THINGS WHICH I DESIRE,

WALKING THROUGH THIS TRIAL OF FIRE.

GOALS I SEEK ARE NOW SET HIGHER,

THIS TIME I WILL TAKE IT TO THE WIRE.

JESUS EXAMPLE I DO ADMIRE,

I AM SINGING HIS PRAISE LIKE A CHOIR.

WORKING FOR GOD I WILL NOT TIRE,

TELLING THAT DEVIL HE IS A LIAR.

REFUGE

COME IN GOD'S CHILDREN OUT
OF THE RAIN BEFORE YOU CATCH A COUGH,
SIT IN FRONT OF MY FIRE PLACE THE
WARMTH WILL DRY YOU OFF.
HAVE SOME TEA AND HONEY OR WOULD YOU
LIKE SOME BROTH,
I GET VISITORS FREQUENTLY IN NEED OF HELP
FOR THEY ARE LOST.
TONIGHT YOU WILL REST IN PEACE THERE IS
SILENCE IN MY LOFT,
FOR I HAVE FLUFFED YOUR PILLOW AND MADE
IT ANGEL SOFT.
WITH MORNING EYES YOU SHALL RISE AND PICK
UP THAT RUGGED CROSS,
IN ALL YOUR WORKS FROM HEAVEN TO EARTH
KNOW THAT JESUS IS
THE BOSS.

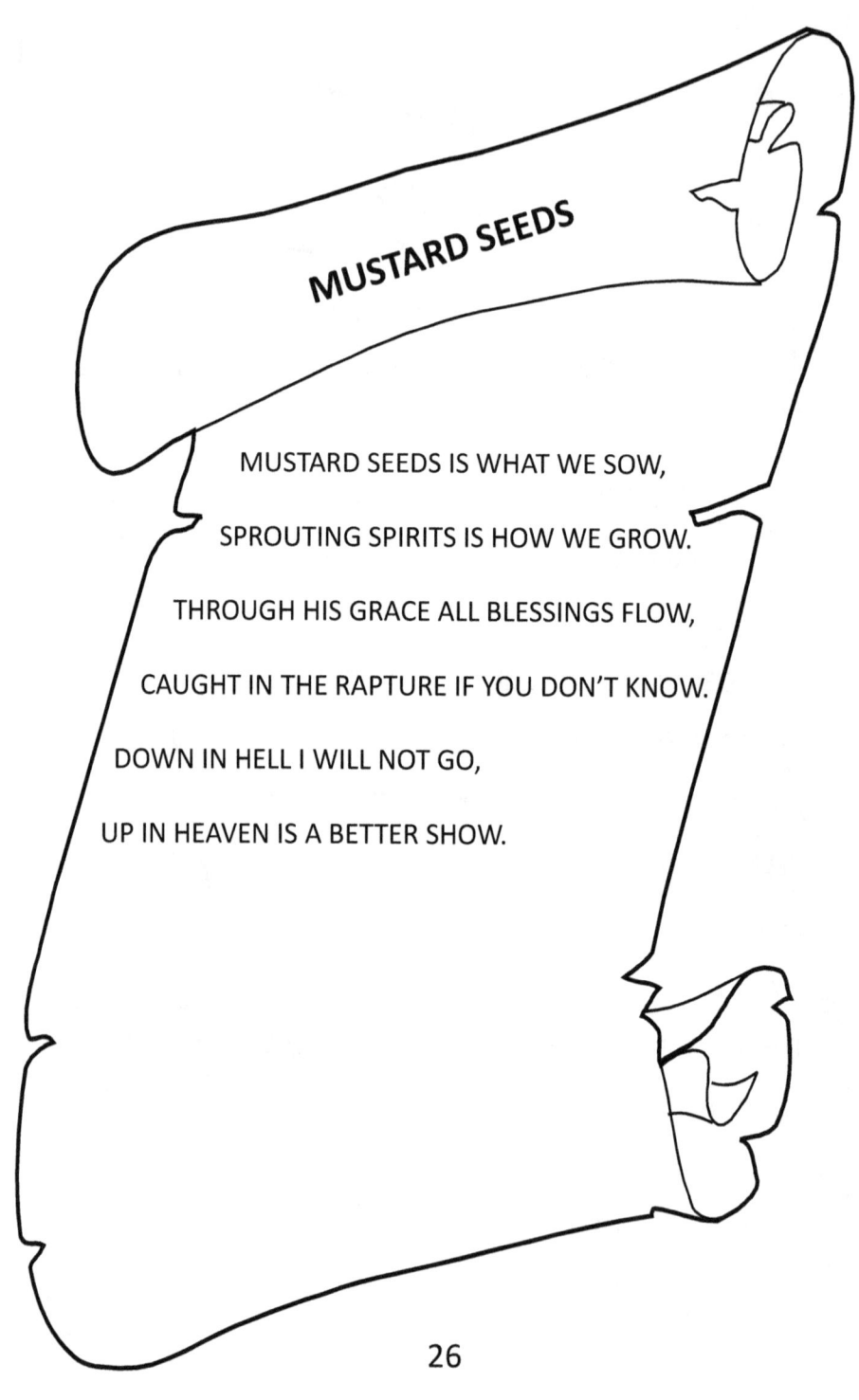

MUSTARD SEEDS

MUSTARD SEEDS IS WHAT WE SOW,

SPROUTING SPIRITS IS HOW WE GROW.

THROUGH HIS GRACE ALL BLESSINGS FLOW,

CAUGHT IN THE RAPTURE IF YOU DON'T KNOW.

DOWN IN HELL I WILL NOT GO,

UP IN HEAVEN IS A BETTER SHOW.

WHAT EVER

WHAT EVER IT IS LORD I WILL DO,

I AM ONLY A SERVANT WHO WORKS FOR YOU.

EVERYTHING FALSE YOU MADE IT TRUE,

YOU WATERED MY FAITH THEN I GREW.

I ONCE BELIEVED THAT I WAS THROUGH,

NOW I AM LIVING A LIFE BRAND NEW.

WHAT YOU SOW

WHAT YOU SOW IS WHAT YOU REAP,

LOCKED IN SHACKLES TO BIND MY FEET.

AN IDOL MIND IS WHERE YOU CREAP,

TO TAKE MY SOUL IS WHAT YOU SEEK.

BEST BELIEVE STILL WATERS RUN DEEP,

I WILL PRAY TO GOD MY SOUL TO KEEP.

I SAY YES

EACH MORNING OF LIFE I SAY YES,

RAIN IN SHOWER I AM FULLY DRESSED.

ANOTHER DAY TO PASS GOD'S TEST,

THROUGH YOUR GRACE NO NEED TO GUESS.

MOVING FORWARD I WILL NOT REST,

OUT FOR GAIN WON'T SETTLE FOR LESS.

IF YOU ARE WONDERING I AM BLESSED,

AND STILL YOU HAVE NOT SEEN MY BEST.

SHARE

SOME PEOPLE SAY THAT LIFE'S NOT FAIR,

NEVER GIVING MORE THAN YOU CAN BARE.

SOMEONE GIVEN WHO REALLY CARES,

UNCONDITIONAL LOVE NOW THAT IS RARE.

TOGETHER FOREVER YOU WILL BE A PAIR,

IN HIS AND HER EYES YOU BOTH WILL STARE.

NEVER THE SELFISH WE ALWAYS SHARE,

FROM OUR BEGINNING JESUS WAS THERE.

MOTHER NATURE

MOTHER NATURE IS ON THE ATTACK,

TRYING TO TAKE HER PLANET BACK.

HOLES IN THE OZONE NOW THAT'S A FACT,

EARTHQUAKES THAT CAUSES THE GROUNDS TO CRACK.

TORNADOS WITHOUT WARNING STRIKES SO FAST,

HURRICANE FORCE WINDS WE PRAY THEY PASS.

THE BIBLE HAS WARNED YOU OF THESE EVENTS,

WHY ASK WHY YOU WERE GIVEN A HINT.

WE ARE LIVING IN THE LAST DAYS,

NO NEED FOR WORRY IF YOU ARE SAVED.

JUST FOR YOU

GREED AND LUST IF WHAT YOU CRAVE,

SELLING THERE SOULS TO BE YOUR SLAVE.

DRINKING AND DRUGGING THEY CALL IT A RAVE,

THINGS THAT LEAD TO A FIRE BALL GRAVE.

WITHOUT A BOAT YOU ARE IN THE WAVE,

DROWNING FAST AND CAN'T BE SAVED.

REACH OUT TO JESUS YOU WILL BE AMAZED,

JUST FOR YOU HIS LIFE HE GAVE.

NOT TOO LATE

IT IS NOT TO LATE FOR YOU TO CROSS OVER,

INVESTIGATE JESUS LIKE YOU WERE MOLDER.

IT DOES NOT MATTER IF YOU ARE YOUNG

OR OLDER,

JOIN GOD'S ARMY AND BE A SOLDIER.

PLEASE WAKE UP AND SMELL THE FOLGER,

SATAN'S LEGIONS ARE GETTING BOLDER.

THERE IS NO WISHING ON A FOUR LEAF CLOVER,

TIMES HAVE CHANGED AND GETTING COLDER.

STAND AND FIGHT

WE ARE THE CHILDREN OF THE LIGHT,

FOLLOWING THE PATHS OF GOOD AND RIGHT.

DARKNESS COMES TO TAKE OUR SIGHT,

BUT WE WON'T GO INTO THE NIGHT.

WITH OUR BROTHERS WE WILL STAND AND FIGHT,

UNTIL THAT DEVIL TAKES A FLIGHT.

MY SAVIOR

LAZARUS WAS RISEN FROM THE DEAD,

ONLY THROUGH ME HIS SAVIOR SAID.

IT TOOK A MIRACLE AND THEY WERE FED,

FILLED WITH FISH AND FIVE LOAVES OF BREAD.

THE APOSTLES WERE WITNESS THAT JESUS LEAD,

BETRAYED BY JUDAS FOR GOLD INSTEAD.

A CROWN OF THORNS AROUND HIS HEAD,

ON CALVARY WAS WHERE MY SAVIOR BLED.

OPEN THE DOORS

OPEN THE DOORS I'M COMING OUT,

HOLY IS THE SPIRIT AND WATCH ME SHOUT.

A KEEPER OF VALUES FROM THE SOUTH,

WISDOM IS WHAT COMES OUT OF MY MOUTH.

WORTHY IS SHE TO BE A SPOUSE,

INCREASING THE VALUE IN HIS HOUSE.

BORN WAS I TO TAKE THIS ROUTE,

NOT OF GOD I DON'T WORRY ABOUT.

HOLY WATER

I AM PLAYING A ROLL THAT HAS BEEN REVERSED,

STARTED OUT LAST BUT NOW I'M FIRST.

EVEN THOUGH THE ENEMY HAS WISHED THE WORST,

BLOW YOUR BUBBLES AND WATCH THEM BURST.

I HAVE BEEN ANOINTED AGAINST SATAN'S EVIL CURSE,

HOLY IS THE WATER THAT QUENCH MY THIRST.

ORIGINAL SIN

DISOBEDIENT TO GOD'S WORD MAN'S ORIGINAL SIN,

THROWN OUT OF PARADISE INTO THE LIONS DEN.

A TRICKLE DOWN AFFECT THAT PLAGUES ITS NEXT OF KIN,

COURTESY OF THE ONE WHO WEARS A DEVILISH GRIN.

BUT JESUS IS ON HIS WAY OPEN YOUR HEART AND LET HIM IN,

IF I NEED TO REPEAT IT I WILL BE HAPPY TO SAY IT AGAIN.

HIS UNDESERVED LOVE HE GAVE FREELY AND FOR ALL MEN,

A FOOL AM I TO LOSE WHEN I HAVE BEEN GIVEN THE MEANS TO WIN.

MORE THAN CONQUERS

THE ESSENCE OF LOVE COMES FROM WITHIN,

REACHING OUT AND CAUSING A TREND.

EVERYONE THAT IS TOUCHED BECOMES A

FRIEND,

EVEN A BROKEN HEART WILL MEND.

LOVE IS COLORLESS ALL WILL BLEND,

THIS IS TRUE NO NEED TO PRETEND.

BONDED TOGETHER TO THE VERY END,

MORE THAN CONQUERS IS WHY YOU'LL WIN.

I ADORE

JESUS IS THE ONE WHOM I ADORE!

I AM IN YOUR ARMS FOREVER MORE.

ENRICHED MY LIFE WHEN IT WAS POOR,

LOVING ME ALL THE WAY TO THE CORE.

COOL IN THE WATERS THAT YOU HAVE POURED,

THE BLESSINGS YOU HAVE GIVEN I CANNOT IGNORE.

ANGELIC WINGS FOR ME TO SOAR,

LIKE THUNDER WHEN YOU HEAR MY ROAR.

POWER

I HAVE THE POWER TO SUCCEED,

WHEN JESUS SUPPLIES ALL MY NEEDS.

HE WILL CUT DOWN ALL YOUR WEEDS,

THEN YOU WILL PLANT AND WATER HIS SEEDS.

WHEN YOU ARE HUNGRY HE WILL FEED,

CROPS ARE PLENTIFUL THERE IS NO GREED.

ON HIS LAND YOU HAVE THE DEED,

FROM THE DRAGON YOU HAVE BEEN FREED.

NO APPEAL

I AM NOT FINISHED ON THE BATTLEFIELD,

SCORCHED MY WINGS BUT THEY WILL HEAL.

THE EATERS OF FLESH WILL HAVE THERE MEAL,

ACCORDING TO THE SCROLLS WITH THE

BROKEN SEAL.

ONCE YOU ARE JUDGED THERE IS NO APPEAL,

BURNING FOREVER IN HELL IS FOR REAL!

NO END

JESUS WILL ALWAYS BE MY FRIEND,

UP IN THE SKY I AM RIDING THE WIND.

OPEN THE GATES AND LET ME IN,

LORD IT IS GOOD TO SEE YOU AGAIN.

I AM HOME FROM WHERE I BEEN,

BLESSED IS HE FOR THERE IS NO END.

CHOSEN

BEFORE I WALKED I HAD TO CRAWL,

A FEW WERE CHOSEN AND MANY ARE CALLED.

UNTIL THE END I WILL GIVE MY ALL,

LEANING ON JESUS IN CASE I FALL.

QUICK IS THE SAND BUT I WON'T STALL,

OVER THE MOUNTAINS NO MATTER HOW TALL.

FOR MY FREEDOM I HAD TO BRAWL,

KNOCKING DOWN MY PRISON WALLS.

TRUST ME

QUESTION, WILL YOU TRUST ME ON THIS?

WORKING FOR JESUS THERE IS NO RISKS.

WHAT ON EARTH WILL YOU EVER MISS,

HEAVEN! IF YOUR NOT ON HIS LIST.

REALITY WILL STRIKE YOU LIKE A FIST,

YOU SHOULD KNOW THAT IGNORANCE IS BLISS.

ALL OF SATAN'S HIGHWAYS HAS A TWIST,

OVER THE EDGE INTO THE ABYSS.

ARE YOU READY

JESUS IS COMING ARE YOU READY,

I AM ENDING THE NIGHTMARE

GOODBYE FREDDY.

I WILL FEAR YOU NOT FOR I AM STEADY,

TURNING MY BACK ON THING'S THAT ARE PETTY.

SPIRITUAL FOOD NOT FOUND IN THE DELI,

THE BODY OF CHRIST TO FILL MY BELLY.

THERE IS NOTHING THAT SATAN CAN TELL ME,

BURNING TO ASHES IS WHAT HELL BE!

NO DEBATE

JESUS IS KING! THERE IS NO DEBATE,

ALWAYS ON TIME HE IS NEVER LATE.

IN HIS HANDS HE HOLDS YOUR FATE,

THIS IS WHY YOU MUST LEARN TO WAIT.

THE DEVIL'S DEAL IS ON THE PLATE,

DO NOT DO SOMETHING THAT YOU WILL HATE.

A CHILD OF GOD YOU CARRY HIS TRAIT,

SERVING THE LORD FOR ME IS GREAT.

LIFE INSURANCE

PUT YOUR CONFIDENCE IN THE LORD,

THERE IS A LIFE INSURANCE YOU CAN AFFORD.

PROTECTION PLAN OF THE DOUBLE EDGE SWORD,

IT HAS BENEFITS AND GREAT REWARDS.

IT IS YOU AND JESUS OF ONE ACCORD,

IMMEDIATE COVERAGE WILL BE ASSURED.

WHAT EVER YOUR SUFFERINGS HAS BEEN CURED,

EVEN AFTER DEATH I AM REASSURED.

BLUEPRINT

WHAT THE BIBLE TEACH WE MUST LEARN,

WITH THE HIGHEST PRIORITY AND

UTMOST CONCERN.

WITHOUT THE BLUEPRINT YOU WILL MAKE

THE WRONG TURN,

OUR CHILDREN WILL LOSE IF WERE NOT STERN.

NOTHING IS FREE IT MUST BE EARNED,

SUBMISSION AND ACCEPTANCE OF JESUS

TERMS.

BUT UNTIL THE DAY OF MY SAVIORS RETURN,

I WILL KEEP MY COOL SO I WON'T BURN.

A SHORT TIME

SATAN KNOWS HIS TIME IS SHORT,

TURN TO JESUS OR YOU WILL BE CAUGHT.

REMEMBER AS CHILDREN WHAT YOU WERE TAUGHT,

DO NOT GIVE THAT DEVIL A SECOND THOUGHT.

IT IS FOOLISH TO GIVE AWAY WHAT WAS BOUGHT,

FOR WANTS AND HAVE AND STILL YOU'LL HAVE NOT.

FINAL PHASE

WE ARE IN THE FINAL PHASE,

DIVIDED TO BE CONQUERED MANY WAYS.

BLINDLY WE ARE WALKING THROUGH A MAZE,

UNABLE TO FIND THE BETTER DAYS.

IN ALL YOU DO GIVE GOD THE PRAISE,

AND DON'T YOU STOP UNTIL THE ROOF IS RAISED.

FOR JESUS I WILL GO OUT IN A BLAZE,

STOMPING MY WAY TO THE GRAVE.

THE ROCK

JESUS IS THE ROCK ON WHICH TO BUILD,

A PLACE OF REST BEYOND THE HILLS.

THERE IS ALWAYS LUMBER IN HIS MILLS,

HE WON'T LEAVE YOU IN THE CHILL.

THERE IS NO REASON YOU CAN'T BE THRILLED,

WHEN ALL YOUR NEEDS HAVE BEEN FILLED.

DID I MENTION THERE IS NO BILL,

GIVEN UNTO YOU IS HIS WILL.

THE FALLEN

ASHES TO ASHES DUST TO DUST,

THOSE WHO HAVE FALLEN WERE THE

ONE'S UNJUST.

LONG TIME AGO THEY WERE JUST LIKE US,

NOW THEY ARE COVERED WITH INIQUITY

AND LUST.

THERE PURIFIED WATERS HAVE TURN TO RUST,

FROM THE BOWLS WHICH THEY EAT NOTHING

BUT CRUST.

WHAT MAKES YOU THINK THAT HELL EQUALS PLUS,

HEAVEN IS NOT HAVING IT AND NEITHER

WILL THE JUST.

THE PLOT

YOU TRIED TO KILL ME THOUGHT I FORGOT,

ONCE WE WERE FRIENDS BUT NOW YOU PLOT.

SWORN TO TAKE EVERYTHING THAT I GOT,

A CONTRACT WAS SIGNED ON THE DOTS.

CONSPIRED WITH DEATH DEALERS TO HAVE ME SHOT,

WHERE NO ONE WOULD FIND ME UNTIL I ROT.

YOU HAVE TRIED TO KEEP ME IN A TIGHT SPOT,

THIS IS JESUS FIGHT YOU THINK IT'S NOT?

HEAR THIS

THIS IS SOMETHING THAT YOU NEED TO HEAR,

WE HAVE COME FROM FAR AND NEAR.

READY FOR WAR IN OUR FULL BATTLE GEAR,

CONTINUING THE FIGHT UNTIL YOUR LEGIONS DISAPPEAR.

APPROVED BY GOD SO THERE IS NOTHING TO FEAR,

STANDING WITH JESUS ONCE THE SMOKE IS CLEAR.

THE VICTORY IS OURS THE ANGELS CHEER,

AND I AM HONORED BECAUSE I WAS THERE.

THE CLAIM

RECLAIMING THAT WHICH WAS STOLEN FROM ME,

LEAVE MY PRESENCE AND LET ME BE.

ONCE WAS BLIND BUT NOW I SEE,

I AM UPLIFTING JESUS UNTIL YOU FLEE.

THINK OF IT AS A DIVORCE DECREE,

LIVING FOR SATAN I WILL NEVER AGREE.

IN THE UPPER ROOM I HAVE A P.H.D.

THERE ARE SO MANY ADVANCEMENTS IN GOD'S INDUSTRY.

CAN'T KEEP ME DOWN

YOU CANNOT KEEP A GOOD MAN DOWN.

HE WILL RISE AGAIN OFF THE GROUND.

HIS MANNERISM IS VERY PROFOUND,

HE IS KNOWN AS A MAN OF GOD IN HIS TOWN.

HIS SENSE OF HUMOR IS THAT OF A CLOWN,

HE IS SUCH A JOY TO HAVE AROUND.

ON HIS FACE THERE IS NEVER A FROWN,

IF YOU LISTEN TO HIS HEART WHAT A

BEAUTIFUL SOUND.

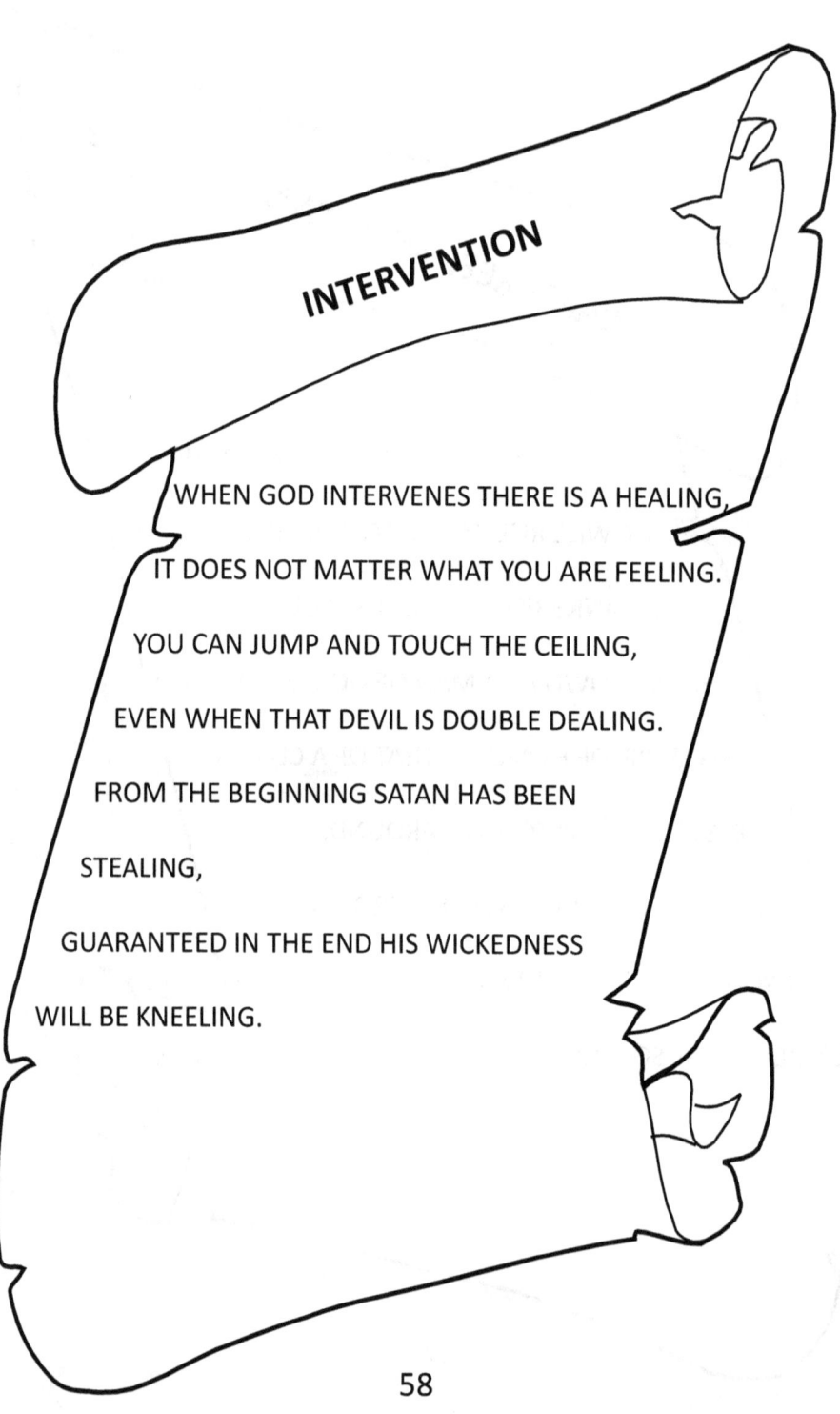

INTERVENTION

WHEN GOD INTERVENES THERE IS A HEALING,

IT DOES NOT MATTER WHAT YOU ARE FEELING.

YOU CAN JUMP AND TOUCH THE CEILING,

EVEN WHEN THAT DEVIL IS DOUBLE DEALING.

FROM THE BEGINNING SATAN HAS BEEN STEALING,

GUARANTEED IN THE END HIS WICKEDNESS WILL BE KNEELING.

PERFECT PEACE

JUST WALK AROUND HEAVEN ALL DAY,

LISTENING TO THE MELODY AS THE

TRUMPETS PLAY.

CRYSTAL CLEAR LIKE THE MONTH OF MAY,

MOLDING FLOWERS THAT'S MADE OF CLAY.

MORNING NOON AND EVENING WE PRAY,

IN PERFECT PEACE IS WHERE WE STAY.

IT NEVER RAINS OR TURN TO GRAY,

REJOICE AND BE HAPPY MY SAVIOR SAY.

WORD OF GOD

THE WORD OF GOD WILL BE TEACHED,

OPEN YOUR HEART AND YOU WILL BE REACHED.

HIS DIRECTIONS IS THE TOPIC THAT'S PREACHED,

RECEIVE WHAT IS GOOD IT TASTE LIKE A PEACH.

ANOINTED WAS JESUS THROUGH EVERY SPEECH,

PUT AN END TO THE SUCKING THE DEVIL IS A LEECH.

DISBARRED

WHEN SATAN WAS IN HEAVEN HE TRIED TO PLAY HARD,

HE WENT AGAINST THE MASTER AND GOT DISBARRED.

DID HE NOT KNOW GOD WOULD PULL HIS CARD,

GOT UPSET AND THE DRAGON WAS SCARRED.

CAST DOWN AND ROAMING IN OUR BACK YARD,

WEAR THE FULL BODY ARMOR AS YOUR GUARD.

RESISTANT TO HEAT YOU WILL NOT BE CHARRED,

IMPERVIOUS TO ATTACK WHEN THE ENEMY BOMBARDS.

YIELD

LORD FOR YOUR GLORY I HAVE YIELD,

YOU ARE WORTHY AND I AM KNEELED.

I REMEMBER WHEN THE DEVIL HAD ME ON MY HEELS,

YOU GAVE ME PROTECTION WITH YOUR SHIELD.

I AM ONLY A FISH AND GOD IS MY REEL,

PULLING ME OUT BEFORE I BECAME A MEAL.

I AM NO LONGER A SLAVE IN SATAN'S FIELD,

I HAVE BEEN BOUGHT AND MY SOUL IS SEALED.

THE TRINITY

TRINITY IS THE FATHER THE SON AND THE HOLY COMBINED,

AND I AM A PRODUCT OF HEAVEN'S DESIGN.

FOR MY SOUL IS ON THE LINE,

THE INTERVENTIONS FROM THE TOP IS DIVINE.

THERE IS NO BOUNDARY WHERE I'LL BE CONFINED,

LIKE A TRANSCENDENT I AM MOVING THROUGH TIME.

NONE OF GOD'S CHILDREN WILL BE LEFT BEHIND,

ALL THAT I HAVE IS THE VICTORY ON MY MIND.

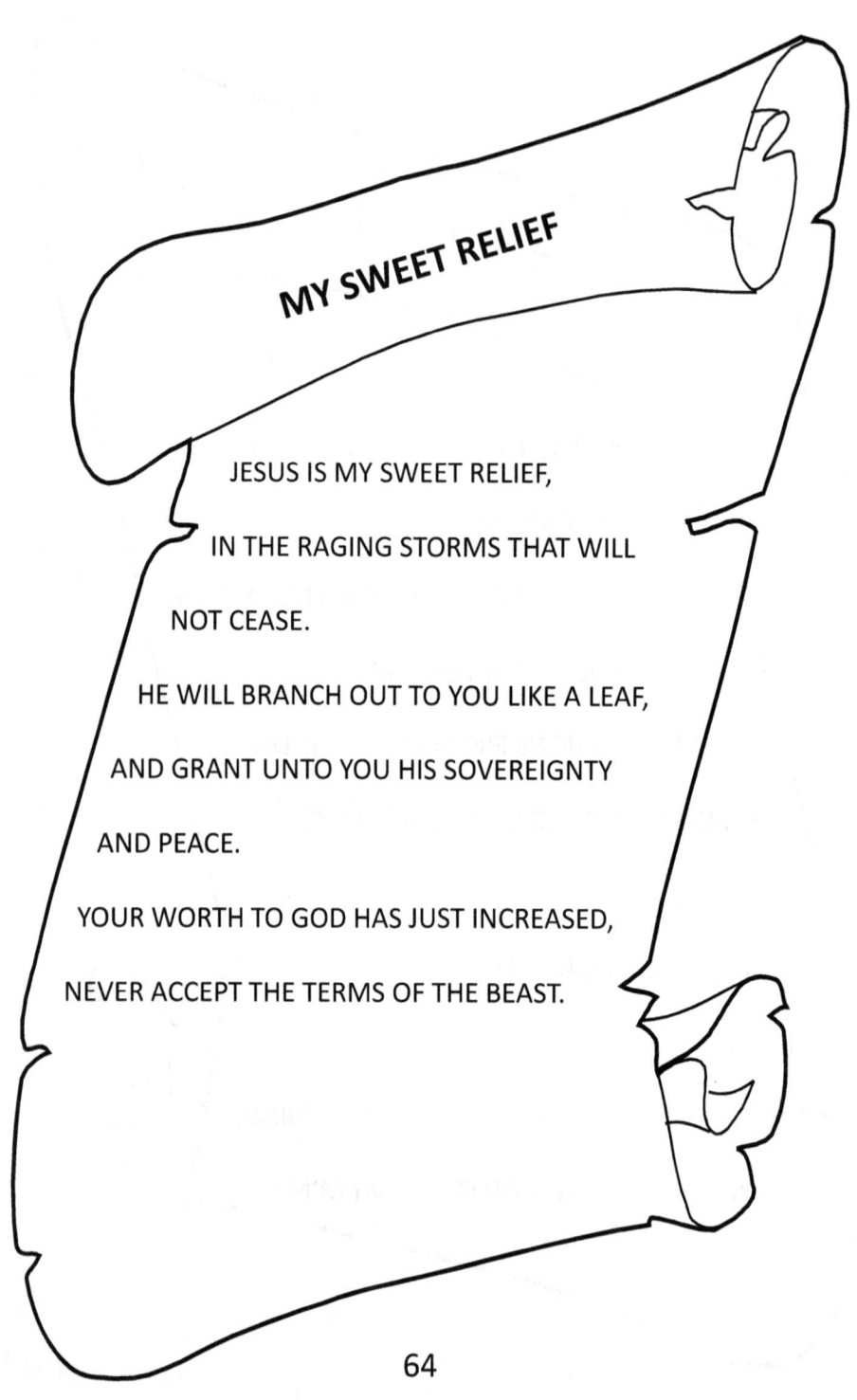

MY SWEET RELIEF

JESUS IS MY SWEET RELIEF,

IN THE RAGING STORMS THAT WILL

NOT CEASE.

HE WILL BRANCH OUT TO YOU LIKE A LEAF,

AND GRANT UNTO YOU HIS SOVEREIGNTY

AND PEACE.

YOUR WORTH TO GOD HAS JUST INCREASED,

NEVER ACCEPT THE TERMS OF THE BEAST.

THE DITCH

I KEPT STRIKING OUT FROM A FAST PITCH,

STILL I WAS A NO HITTER WHEN THEY SWITCH.

DEEPER I AM SINKING IN THIS DITCH,

FEELS LIKE I'M UNDER THE SPELL OF A WITCH.

THE BLEEDING HAS STOPPED AND GOD IS MY STITCH,

BUT I AM REMINDED EACH TIME IT ITCH.

IF JESUS IS GOING I WILL BE HITCHED,

AND THERE IS NO MISHAPS ERRORS OR GLITCH.

THE ZONE

SATAN YOUR COVER HAS BEEN BLOWN,

YOUR HIDDEN AGENDAS EVEN THEY

ARE KNOWN.

STRATEGICALLY WE HAVE BEEN PLACED

INSIDE A ZONE,

EASILY ACCESSED TO THE FLESH AND BONE.

FROM OUR BIRTH UNTIL WE ARE GROWN,

THE LIFE WE LIVE IS IT REALLY OUR OWN?

MY SAFETY NET

JESUS YOU ARE MY SAFETY NET,

FOR MY SOUL HE HAS ERASED MY DEBT.

HE COMES IN A HURRY LIKE A JET,

AND DRIED ME OFF WHEN I WAS WET.

HE WILL DO IT FOR YOU IF YOU LET,

MY MONEY IS ON JESUS AND I DON'T BET.

THE ABUNDANCE OF LIFE IS WHAT YOU GET,

AND THAT'S A GUARANTEE FROM THE OLDEST VET.

IF YOU KNOCK

THE DOORS WILL OPEN IF YOU KNOCK,

ALL ARE WELCOME IT IS NEVER LOCKED.

TAKE THIS TIME TO PURCHASE HIS STOCK,

EVERYONE SHOULD HAVE A PIECE OF THE ROCK.

I WILL ADMIT I AM ONE OF HIS FLOCK,

NEVER BEFORE TO HAVE A BLESSING BLOCKED.

MY SHIP ALWAYS COME STRAIGHT TO MY DOCK,

AND IT IS ALWAYS ON TIME BY MY CLOCK.

A TOWER

RESIST THE DEVIL YOU HAVE THE POWER,

THIS CHILD OF GOD WILL NOT BE DEVOUR.

JESUS WILL COME IN THE MIDNIGHT HOUR,

TO SHINE HIS LIGHT ON A FALLEN FLOWER.

HE CAN MAKE BUTTERMILK SWEET WHEN

YOUR MILK TURNS SOUR,

AND HE CAN BUILD YOU UP AGAIN TO STAND

LIKE A TOWER.

THE FOUNTAIN

ALLOW ME THIS MOMENT TO BE FRANK,

PROSPERITY YOU HAVE GOD TO THANK.

IT IS LIKE HAVING MONEY IN THE BANK,

BECAUSE YOUR BALANCE IS NEVER A BLANK.

JESUS IS THE FOUNTAIN FROM WHICH I DRANK,

AND I AM A SOLDIER WITH THE HIGHEST RANK.

GOD WON'T ALLOW YOU TO WALK THE PLANK,

BUT GIVE YOU THE POWER AND THE STRENGTH

OF A TANK.

ASCENSION

THE RIGHT OF ASCENSION WAS APPOINTED BY JOHN,
SUBMERGED BENEATH THE SURFACE IN SUBMISSION TO THE POND.
ARISE KING JESUS FOR YOU HAVE COMPLETED THE HOLY BOND,
ALL ANGELS BOWED AT FIRST LIGHT OF HEAVEN'S DAWN.
THE ONE CALLED HORNSWOGGLE IS A LIAR AND A CON,
WITH A DIRTY BAG OF TRICKS HE'S A PRETENDER OF A MAGIC WAND.
THE OUR FATHER PRAYER I PRAY THIS JUST BEFORE I YAWN,
JESUS SOIL COMES FERTILIZED SO THE GREENER IS MY LAWN.

THE GAME

SATAN IS THE MASTER OF THE GAME,

ONCE IN PLAY YOU WILL TAKE THE BLAME.

I AM MUD WILL BE YOUR NAME,

TOOK A BAD PICTURE IN THE FRAME.

AGAINST THE DEVIL YOU MUST TAKE AIM,

HIS APPETITE FOR DESTRUCTION IS STILL THE

SAME.

PLEASE WISE UP YOUR EXCUSES ARE LAME,

THESE ARE SOME OF THE REASONS OUR SAVIOR

CAME.

REDEMPTION

THIS IS SOMETHING I FORGOT TO MENTION,

THERE IS NO MAN THAT IS BEYOND REDEMPTION.

YOU MUST FIRST GIVE GOD ALL OF YOUR ATTENTION,

AND ALL YOUR SINS MUST BE AN ADMISSION.

YOUR HEART WILL BE SEARCHED THROUGH IT'S ENCRYPTION,

FOR GOD KNOWS ALL OF YOUR INTENTIONS.

YOU ARE NOW A BRAND NEW INVENTION,

FAR AND AWAY FROM THE DEVIL'S HINCHMAN.

INSURRECTION

GOD FAVORED MAN THIS WAS NOT A REJECTION,

BUT JEALOUSY WAS THE REASON FOR SATAN'S INSURRECTION.

ASSEMBLED AND ATTACKED WITH A THIRD OF HIS AGGRESSION,

NO LONGER IN HEAVEN DO YOU HAVE A CONNECTION.

YOU CAN'T EVEN LOOK AT YOUR OWN REFLECTION,

KNOWING THAT ONCE YOU WERE HEAVEN'S FIRST SELECTION.

NOW ALL YOU ARE IS A NASTY INFECTION,

ONLY A FOOL WOULD FOLLOW YOUR DIRECTION.

CIRCUS MONKEY

DO NOT BE THE DEVIL'S CIRCUS MONKEY,

HE IS JUST USING YOU LIKE A JUNKY.

AN EMPTY CONTAINER MAKES YOU A DUMMY,

JUST PUT ON YOUR CAP THAT READS SATAN'S

FLUNKY.

HE WILL WRAP YOU UP LIKE AN ANCIENT

MUMMY,

AND FEED YOU GARBAGE BUT YOU WILL THINK

IT'S YUMMY.

DO YOU NOT REMEMBER THE EGG NAME HUMPTY,

IF YOU WAKE UP IN HELL YOU'LL REALLY BE

GRUMPY.

ALPHA AND OMEGA

YOU ARE ONCE AGAIN WITNESS TO A SPIRITUAL PRODUCTION,

GIVING PRAISE AND HONOR TO THE ONE WHO NEEDS NO INTRODUCTION.

HE IS THE ALPHA AND OMEGA OF THIS DISCUSSION,

BRACE YOURSELF FOR THE HOLY ERUPTION.

FEEL THE IMPACT SATAN OF YOUR CONCUSSION,

I WILL ONLY FOLLOW MY SAVIOR'S INSTRUCTIONS.

GOD CLEARED MY PATH OF ALL YOUR OBSTRUCTIONS,

AND PUT MY HOUSE UNDER HEAVEN'S CONSTRUCTION.

ENDORSEMENT

MY SERVICE TO GOD HAS BEEN ENDORSE,

MAKE NO MISTAKE I'M COMING WITH FULL FORCE.

HERE IS YOUR CHANCE TO CHANGE YOUR COURSE,

I WILL STOMP OUT THE DEVIL WITH NO REMORSE.

CHOOSE GOD NOW HE WILL GRANT YOUR RECOURSE,

CHOOSE GOD NOT ETERNAL DAMN NATION WILL BE ENFORCED!

A LAMP

THE ROADS WERE LONG AND VERY DAMP,

THIS IS MY TIME I AM WALKING THE RAMP.

IT'S A KNOCKOUT WE HAVE A NEW CHAMP,

ALL THANKS TO GOD AND HIS ELITE CAMP.

IN HEAVEN AND ON EARTH THE CROWD IS AMP,

THE VICTORY IS APPROVED I HAVE HIS STAMP.

I HELD ON TO JESUS WITH JUST A CLAMP,

THEN I FOUND THE TUNNEL WITH AN

ILLUMINATING LAMP.

TICKING DOWN

TWO THOUSAND YEARS AGO A SAVIOR WAS SENT,

TODAY SOME ARE STILL IGNORANT TO WHAT THAT MEANT.

TO LOVE THY NEIGHBOR I WONDER WHERE THIS WENT,

LORD HAVE MERCY HOW AM I GONNA PAY MY RENT.

TICKING DOWN CLOCKS TO THE MAIN EVENT,

WITH WHOM WAS YOUR TIME MOSTLY SPENT.

ALL WILL BE FORGIVEN IF YOU REPENT,

YOU MUST DO IT QUICKLY BEFORE JESUS DESCENT.

MY QUARTERBACK

WHEN SATAN PLANS HIS ALL OUT ATTACK,

I HAVE JESUS AS MY QUARTERBACK!

NEVER WILL JESUS EVER TAKE A SACK,

THAT IS WHY I'M RIDING ON HIS BACK.

EVEN WHEN THE ODDS ARE GREATLY STACK,

NOT ONE OF HIS OWN WILL EVER LACK.

IF ALL YOU CAN SEE IS WHITE AND BLACK,

BEST BELIEVE YOU ARE ON THE WRONG TRACK.

THE PURPOSAL

KILLING EACH OTHER SHOULD NOT BE THE

WAY IT GOES,

MAKE LOVE AND NOT WAR IS WHAT I PURPOSE.

INSTEAD OF GUN FIRE WOULD YOU EXCHANGE

A ROSE,

BUT I GUESS THAT IS BEING SILLY I SUPPOSE.

HOW CAN WE UNITE IF WE REMAIN FOES,

FROM THE FIRST CASUALTY NOTHING BUT WOES.

WILL ALL SIDES AGREE THIS MATTER IS CLOSED,

AND THE IMMEDIATE EXTRACTION OF OUR G.I. JOES

A JEWEL

THE PEOPLE IN THIS WORLD CAN BE VERY CRUEL,

BUT GOD WILL USE YOU AS HIS TOOL.

ON EARTH WE ARE GOVERN BY SATAN'S RULE,

AND WITH THAT IN MIND DON'T BE HIS FOOL.

YOU WERE TAUGHT TO LOVE SINCE BIBLE SCHOOL,

YOU ARE PRECIOUS TO JESUS LIKE A JEWEL.

ROAD BLOCKS WILL BE TURNED INTO A STEPPING STOOL,

THE MASTER YOUR SERVING IS HE THIS COOL?

THE SHOWDOWN

WELCOME TO THE SHOWDOWN IT
IS SCHEDULED FOR HIGH NOON,
BUT THIS IS NO WESTERN OR QUICK
DRAW SALOON.
IF YOUR READY TO TAKE AIM THEN FIRE YOUR
HARPOON,
WHILE YOUR MIND IS TRANSFORMING YOU
CAN BEND THE SPOON.
THE METAMORPHOSIS IS COMPLETE COME
OUT OF YOUR CACOON,
YOU'VE BEEN CHANGED BY THE ONE WHO IS
HIGHER THAN THE MOON.
HOW SWEET IS THE SOUND OF
A BRAND NEW TUNE,
FOR THOSE WHO ARE GODLY YOUR
TIME IS SOON.

HOPE

THEY LAID MY KING INSIDE A TOMB,

HAVE MERCY ON US FOR WE ARE DOOM.

ON THE THIRD DAY THERE WAS A SILENT BOOM,

OUR LORD AND SAVIOR HAS LEFT THE ROOM.

JESUS HAS RISEN IS WHAT THE MINORITY ASSUMED,

NOW THERE IS HOPE IN YOUR TIMES OF GLOOM.

SUPERNATURAL

INCORPORATE THE VISION THAT IS BEYOND THE NORM,

STEP OUT OF THE NATURAL INTO A SUPERNATURAL FORM.

EMBRACE THE BAD WEATHER AND BECOME A STORM,

A MIGHTY RIVER RAGING AND I AM JUST GETTING WARM.

THIS FLESH I WEAR IS GETTING OLD AND WORN.

MY SPIRIT IS MORE THAN A MATCH AGAINST THE ENEMY SWORM.

THE REBIRTH

JESUS IS MY FATHER AND I AM
PROUD TO BE HIS SON,
NO LONGER AM I AFRAID SATAN NO
LONGER WILL I RUN.
THE BLASPHEMER OF ALL SACRED THINGS
I KNOW NOW HOW YOU COME,
THE ANTI-CHRIST WITH A HEART OF ICE
MANIPULATING JUST FOR FUN.
THE REBIRTH IS AN EXPLOSION THAT HAS
LEFT THE ENEMY STUN,
THERE IS NO MISTAKE THAT GOD WILL MAKE
TO CHOOSE ME AS THE ONE.
YOU SENT ALL OF HELL TO STOP ME YOU
DEVIL BEFORE MY JOB BEGUN,
SEALED IS YOUR FATE YOUR TO LATE THE
PROPHECY AND HIS WILL
BE DONE.

SONGS OF THE SURVIVOR

GOD INSPIRED THE SONGS OF THE SURVIVOR,

WRITTEN WITH THE HOPES OF MAKING

YOU WISER.

IF YOU JUST REMEMBER THAT JESUS IS

THE DRIVER,

HE WILL STEER YOU CLEAR OF THE

UNDERHANDED CONNIVER.

TALK WITH GOD HE IS AN EXCELLENT ADVISOR,

AGAINST THE ENEMY HE IS ALSO A NEUTRALIZER.

YOU ALREADY KNOW THAT SATAN IS A LIAR,

TRUST NO MISTAKE A BURNT CHILD DRED FIRE.

HOT LINE

THERE IS A TWENTY-FOUR HOUR HOT LINE THAT YOU CAN DIAL,
ON THE OTHER END IS JESUS WAITING TO TALK FOR A WHILE.
HAVING A FRIEND LIKE THIS REALLY MAKES ME SMILE,
HE WILL ALSO HELP YOU TO GO THAT EXTRA MILE.
DON'T HATE MY MASTER WHEN YOURS HAS NO STYLE,
AND I AM NOT EVEN CONCERN IF I MAKE THE ENEMY RILE.
ALL ACTS OF SATAN'S TREACHERY WE HAVE ON FILE,
A UNANIMOUS VERDICT OF GUILTY IN THE DEVIL'S TRIAL.

INDEPENDENCE

YOU HAVE BEEN ASKING FOR GOD TO GIVE YOU A BREAK,

INDEPENDENCE IS YOURS IF YOU WISH IT TO TAKE.

SEVER THE HEAD OF THE SLITHERY SNAKE,

TOSS IT IN THE FIRE AND WATCH IT BAKE.

YOU HAVE BEEN GIVEN THE PADDLES TO ROW HIS LAKE,

PLEASE DO NOT LOSE THEM FOR HEAVEN'S SAKE.

FROM HERE ON OUT HAPPINESS IS WHAT YOU MAKE,

LIFE CAN BE FILLED WITH PLEASANTRIES WITHOUT THE ACHE.

THE SURVEY

ATTENTION HOMOSAPIENS HERE IS A SURVEY JUST FOR YOU,

THE BEAST THAT KILLS HIMSELF HAS PUT THE ANIMALS IN THE ZOO.

FIRST BLOOD WAS MY BROTHER NOT EVEN AN ENEMY THAT HE SLEW,

TRANSFUSING THROUGHOUT TIME LEAVING A TRANSMITTING RESIDUE.

BUT FULL OF FAITH IS THE FAITHFUL KNOWING THAT EARTH WILL BE ANEW,

ONCE MORE AGAIN PARADISE AND YOU CAN HAVE IT TOO.

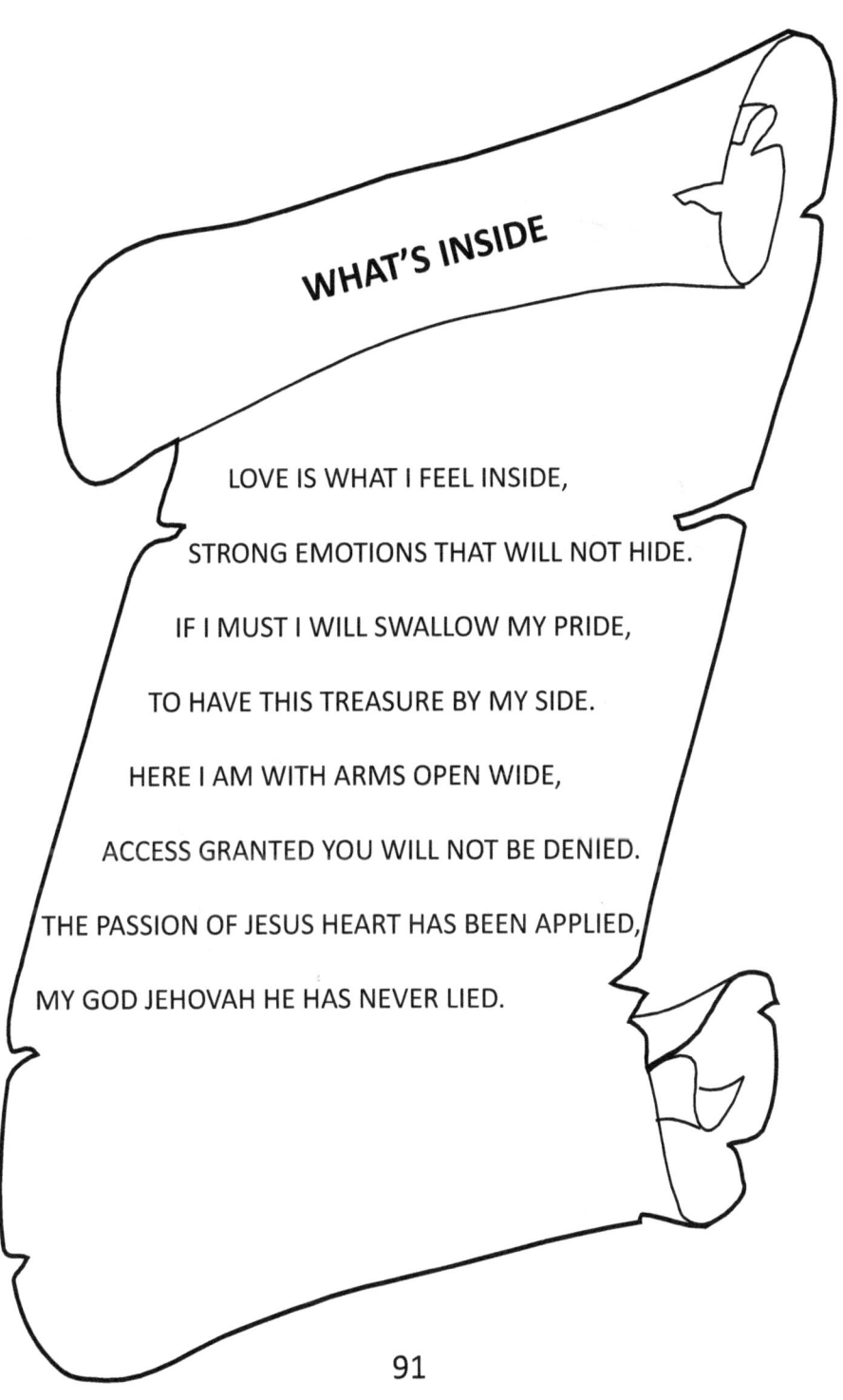

WHAT'S INSIDE

LOVE IS WHAT I FEEL INSIDE,

STRONG EMOTIONS THAT WILL NOT HIDE.

IF I MUST I WILL SWALLOW MY PRIDE,

TO HAVE THIS TREASURE BY MY SIDE.

HERE I AM WITH ARMS OPEN WIDE,

ACCESS GRANTED YOU WILL NOT BE DENIED.

THE PASSION OF JESUS HEART HAS BEEN APPLIED,

MY GOD JEHOVAH HE HAS NEVER LIED.

PERFECT

MANIFESTED ON EARTH WAS THE HISTORICAL LOCATION,

IN THE CITY OF DAVID WAS THE BLESSED CORONATION.

WELCOME THE MESSIAH THE KING OF ALL NATIONS,

THE ONLY SOURCE OF PRESERVATION FOR YOUR SALVATION.

THREE-HUNDRED AND SIXTY FIVE DAYS YOU ARE IN HIS ROTATION,

HE IS THE PERFECT ANSWER TO ALL YOUR SITUATIONS.

COUNTER CLOCK

TICK TOCK TICKING COUNTER CLOCK WISE,

IS THE ONE WHO HAS DECEIVED YOU

THE ONE WHO TELL LIES.

PLEASE DON'T ACT LIKE THIS IS SUCH A

SURPRISE,

WHAT HAS HARDEN YOUR HEART ALSO HAS

BLINDED YOUR EYES.

THIS WORLDLY OBSESSION YOU MUST BREAK

THESE TIES,

DO OR DO NOT BUT THERE IS NO TRY.

FOR THE WORD HAS BEEN GIVEN OF SATAN'S

DEMISE,

ARE YOU STILL NOT CONVINCED THAT JESUS

IS ALIVE?

A JOURNEY

WHY DO YOU CRY THY WEEPING CHILD,

FOR I AM HOME ACROSS THE NILE.

A JOURNEY WHICH I TRAVELED OVER A

MILLION MILES,

HIS KNOWLEDGE HIS WISDOM AND

UNDERSTANDING COMPILED.

NO LONGER TO BE A STUDENT BUT A MASTER

IN HIS TRIALS,

WRITTEN WHEN JEHOVAH CONSTRUCTED THE

HALLS OF HEAVEN'S AISLES.

NOT ALONE

THE BUTTON HAS BEEN PUSHED AND I AM IN YOUR ZONE,

BORN AGAIN IS THE SPIRIT AND THIS TEST IS ON.

LIKE TONY JAH AND I AM BAD TO THE BONE,

ALL THAT I GOT STRAIGHT TO YOUR DOME.

I WILL NEVER STOP FIGHTING UNTIL THE DAY YOUR GONE,

THIS SOUTHERN STYLE WHIPPING K-TOWN HOME GROWN.

WITH EASE I WILL BREEZE YOUR HEAD IS FLOWN,

THY ROD AND THY STAFF FOR I AM NOT ALONE.

THE FAST LANES

GET OUT OF THE FAST LANES
AND WAVE THE CAUTION FLAG,
HAVE FAITH IN THE TORTOISE HE WILL
OUT LAST THE JAG.
IT'S A DOG EAT DOG WORLD BUT YOU CAN LET
YOUR TAIL WAG,
A LIVE CHICKEN BEATS A DEAD DUCK STUFFED
IN A BODY BAG.
THE ADVICE OF TRUE LIFE CAN SAVE YOUR LIFE
DON'T TAKE IT AS A NAG,
PULL UP YOUR PANTS SO YOU CAN DANCE
SLOPPY IS YOUR SAG.
FROM HIDE AND SEEK TO UP THE CREEK ORANGE
SUITS WITHOUT A TAG,
A REAL MAN IS A GODLY MAN AND ON HIM
HIS FAMILY BRAG.

SIGHT BEYOND SIGHT

WHAT A GIFT FROM GOD TO HAVE SIGHT BEYOND SIGHT,

HIS POWERS OF PERCEPTION THAT NEEDS NO LIGHT.

CLIMB THE MOUNTAIN AND YOU WILL REACH THIS HEIGHT,

YOUR STEPS WILL BE ORDERED FROM WRONG TO RIGHT.

UNKNOWN TO MANY IS GOD'S POWER AND MIGHT,

NOW I AM A SPIRITUAL WATCHER TO HIS DELIGHT.

THE SOLUTION

BELIEVE NOTHING OF WHAT YOU SEE IT IS KNOWN AS AN OPTICAL ILLUSION, CONTRARY TO THE FACT THE TRUTH IS THAT WE ARE LIVING AN ORCHESTRATED DELUSION.

WHO REALLY CARES IF I TAKE YOU THERE PLEASE PARDON MY INTRUSION,

JUST THINK FOR A MINUTE IF I'M DEAD CAN I SPEND IT.

I HOPE THAT IS NOT YOUR CONCLUSION.

WITHOUT JEHOVAH TO CARRY YOU OVER YOU WILL BE LOST IN HELL'S CONFUSION,

BUT YOU CAN SAY FROM HERE TODAY THAT JESUS IS MY SOLUTION.

OUT HOUSE

WELCOME TO HELL'S OUT HOUSE THIS COULD BE YOUR FINAL LEVEL,

IF YOU DID NOT SERVE GOD YOU WERE SERVING THE DEVIL.

ONCE YOU ARE BURIED IN THE EARTH THERE IS NO NEED FOR A SHOVEL,

THIS IS JUST A WARNING TO ALL YOU RUNNING REBELS.

HAVE YOU HAD ENOUGH BASS ALLOW ME TO TURN UP THE TREBLE,

A DOLLAR FOR YOU SOUL I FIND THIS MOST INCREDIBLE.

NOT PROMISED

TOMORROW IS NOT PROMISED BUT IT IS NOT TO LATE TODAY,

ACKNOWLEDGE JESUS AS YOUR SAVIOR THAT IS ALL YOU NEED TO SAY.

AS CHILDREN OF GOD WHEN TIMES ARE HARD IN TRUTH IS HOW WE PRAY,

TO FIND THE ROAD THAT LEADS US HOME I AM FINALLY ON MY WAY.

THE LESSONS I LEARNED WERE VERY STERN THANK YOU FOR ESSIE MAE,

TO SOON TO LEAVE ME GREAT GRANDMA PHOEBE I HAVE MISSED YOU EVERYDAY.

www.ingramcontent.com/pod-product-compliance
Lightning Source LLC
Chambersburg PA
CBHW050652160426
43194CB00010B/1913